The Art of the Band T-shirt

The Art of the Band T-shirt

**Amber Easby &
Henry Oliver**

POCKET
BOOKS

First published in the USA by Simon & Schuster Inc., 2007
First published in Great Britain by Pocket Books, 2007
An imprint of Simon & Schuster UK Ltd, A CBS Company

1 3 5 7 9 10 8 6 4 2

Simon & Schuster UK Ltd, Africa House, 64–78 Kingsway, London WC2B 6AH

www.simonsays.co.uk

Simon & Schuster Australia, Sydney

A CIP catalogue for this book is available from the British Library.

ISBN-10: 1-84739-073-0
ISBN-13: 978-1-84739-073-8

Additional design by Jeff Sheinkopf
Additional interviews by Ben Blackwell
Flaming Lips, Mudhoney "Soft Hell", and Melvins "Fiend Club" photographs by Geoff Peveto
Yes photographs by Roger Dean
Minor Threat, Dischord, and Fugazi photographs by Jeff Nelson
The Allman Brothers Band photographs by Kirk West, except "Enlightened Rogues"

Designed by Jane Archer
Printed and bound in Great Britain by CPI Bath

For our parents

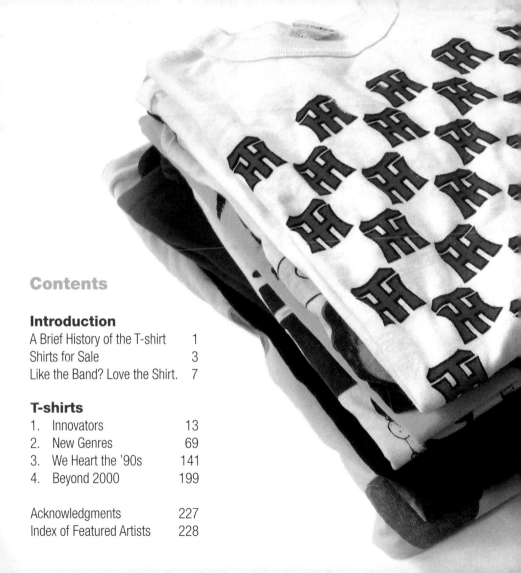

Contents

Introduction

T-shirts

A Brief History of the T-shirt

Like most histories, the history of the T-shirt is full of parallel stories and competing points of view. Both U.S. and British navies, among others, claim its origins. Some claim that the T-shirt was conceived in the 1880s by the U.S. Navy. The uniform included a white button-up flannelette undershirt that was often worn by itself once the ship was out to sea, and sailors required clothing more flexible and comfortable than their standard uniforms to perform more laborious tasks. Although there had been button-up flannelette underwear for years, this is often thought of as the first "official" outing of undergarments worn as overwear.

Around the same time on the other side of the Atlantic, others claim that the T-shirt had its origin in the woolen singlets of the British Royal Navy. The story goes that upon hearing that Queen Victoria would make a surprise inspection, an officer noticed that the singlets failed to cover up the sailors' tattoos and ordered that sleeves be added to the garment to cover them up for the royal visit. Although this seems a little ridiculous and no real documents of the visit seem to have been found, the legend lives on.

What is certain, though, is that in 1913 the U.S. Navy officially added to its uniform a buttonless, woolen crew neck undershirt. According to many, it was during the First World War that the U.S. soldiers noticed that the lighter cotton undershirts worn by the French soldiers were cooler in the summer and dried more quickly in the winter. The cotton T-shirt was on its way.

While gaining steady momentum throughout the 1930s, the T-shirt received a major setback in the film *It Happened One Night* when Clark Gable took off his shirt to reveal no undershirt at all. Women throughout the United States loved the look of the bare chest, and men across the country followed suit by wearing nothing under their shirts. But the T-shirt's resilient popularity recovered and began to populate mail-order catalogues nationwide. In 1938 Fruit of the Loom and Hanes both started mass manufacturing T-shirts, and Sears, Roebuck and Co. advertised its "gob" shirt as an under- or outer garment and priced it at twenty-four cents.

By the Second World War, the T-shirt was standard issue in both the army and the navy. Its military usage made the T-shirt a symbol of masculinity and strength while still being comfortable and versatile. As World War Two spread to the heat of the Pacific, the T-shirt became the predominant uniform of U.S. soldiers. While the white T-shirts were suitable for life in the navy, army soldiers soon realized the white T-shirts made them an easily visible target, so they dyed their shirts with coffee grinds until the Army brought in sage-green T-shirts late in the war.

Media coverage of the war beamed images of these soldiers into households nationwide, giving much of the country their first look at what would soon be the most popular clothing in the world. It was also during the war that soldiers began to print their own T-shirts. Using screen printing and stenciling for the first time made T-shirts as much a message board as a piece of clothing. Soldiers would print T-shirts with their station post, corps, or point of origin. In 1942 a *Life* magazine cover featured a muscular soldier, gun in hand, ready for action, proudly wearing a T-shirt with the print "Air Corps Gunnery School Las Vegas Nevada." It was with this cover that the future of the humble T-shirt became apparent.

In the 1950s the T-shirt really came into its own. In the 1951 film *A Streetcar Named Desire,* Marlon Brando showed the world his physique in a tight-fitting white T-shirt. This perpetuated the T-shirt's shift from hiding under the shirt to being the shirt, and it was only going to get more popular. In 1953 Brando again sported the new jeans-and-T-shirt look in the film *The Wild One*, and in 1955 teenagers found their hero in James Dean's portrayal of a disaffected youth in Nicholas Ray's *Rebel Without a Cause*. *Rebel Without a Cause* quickly made the T-shirt a symbol of the new generation. No longer just young adults, children in smaller versions of their parents' clothes, these teenagers were the epitome of new American youth. Young people with disposable income and disposable time made a culture for themselves that their parents could not understand. They rode motorcycles, listened to rock-'n'-roll music, and struggled to find their place in the quiet of a postwar suburban society. The T-shirt was their uniform.

In the late 1950s and early 1960s the T-shirt underwent major changes—in form and in function. In its liberation from the underwear section, the T-shirt became a heavier, more substantial piece of clothing. Sleeves became longer, neckholes became smaller, and the cotton became heavier and more durable. But more important than the physical change the T-shirt underwent was the major change in the idea of the T-shirt. The blank canvas of a crisp white T-shirt soon inspired savvy marketers to use the T-shirt as an advertising space that was not only cheap to produce but was also extremely mobile and visible. T-shirts became souvenirs used by everyone from America's biggest corporations to the local garage around the corner. The stage was set. Soon Elvis Presley would be offering T-shirts to his fans so they could show their love for rock-'n'-roll's first superstar. And it was only a matter of time before the T-shirt would fulfill its ultimate potential as a piece of memorabilia: the rock concert T-shirt.

Shirts for Sale

An Elvis T-shirt from 1956 is the earliest example available. This period is so early in the life of the band T-shirt that we can only speculate that the shirt may have been sold through a fan club or used promotionally.

Rin Tanaka, author of the cult *My Freedamn* series, credits The Monkees as the first band to have their own successful merchandising company, and apparently they sold T-shirts on their first U.S. tour in 1967. However, the Beatles had T-shirts for sale three years earlier, during their first tour of the United States in 1964.

The Beatles' manager, Brian Epstein, licensed their merchandising rights earlier that year to Nicky Byrne for a measly 10 percent of the profits. Byrne started two companies, Stramsact in the United Kingdom and Seltaeb in the United States, to fulfill the overwhelming requests. According to Craig Cross, author of *The Beatles: Day-by-Day, Song-by-Song, Record-by-Record*, an American T-shirt company paid Byrne the relatively low licensing fee of one hundred thousand dollars and sold one million shirts in the first three days of business. Tony Barrow, the Beatles' publicist from 1963 to 1968, said, "In merchandising terms, the only possible comparison was Walt Disney. In pop, nothing had ever been that big." Epstein immediately regretted his decision and attempted to renegotiate the contract. Three years later, after a multitude of lawsuits, the deal was settled out of court. Cross wrote, "Even if the Beatles weren't the first band to profit from merchandising, they were certainly the first band to be ripped off by it. They lost millions!"

While Elvis Presley, the Beatles, and the Monkees all participated in early music merchandising, the T-shirt was one of many products for sale in their names. The Beatles had everything from candy bars to alarm clocks and board games to lunch boxes. Along with Ringo wigs and toothbrushes, T-shirts were considered another fad. The fixture of the concert or tour shirt—a T-shirt specifically manufactured for a special event or series of shows—has been widely attributed to promoter and entrepreneur Bill Graham.

In 1965 Graham began promoting shows for acts such as the Steve Miller Band, Jefferson Airplane, Janis Joplin, and the Grateful Dead. He founded the Fillmore (which relocated and was renamed the Fillmore West) in San Francisco and the Fillmore East in New York City. Graham was also an early champion of psychedelic art, commissioning artists to make posters for his concerts. In 1971 he leased the Winterland Arena, setting the standard for large-production arena rock shows.

Ira Sokoloff worked as an advertising agent for promoters Jimmy Koplik and Shelly Finkel of Cross Country Concerts, who asked him to design a full-page ad to place in the *Village Voice*. The ad was for the Allman Brothers' performance at the Nassau Coliseum in Long Island on May 1, 1973. Sokoloff decided to print the ad on a dozen shirts as a gift for the band and its management. The band loved the shirts so much that they asked Sokoloff to sell them at the show. Sokoloff does not remember how many T-shirts they sold that night, but he recalls that they "were all pleasantly surprised."

The Summer Jam at Watkins Glen, New

York, was held on July 28, 1973. The infamous festival attracted six hundred thousand fans and featured marathon performances by the Band, the Grateful Dead, and the Allman Brothers. Koplik and Finkel organized the festival, although Graham provided the extra speakers needed to accommodate the colossal crowd. Sokoloff was there selling T-shirts that he made specifically for the concert. On the front of the shirt was a logo that he had designed to represent the three bands on the bill. On the back was the name of each act. He customized a shirt for Graham as a gift, adding Graham's name to the shirt. It was soon after that Graham started making shirts for every concert and tour he promoted. Graham's company, Winterland Productions, went on to become one of the most prominent merchandising companies in the United States.

Until this time, T-shirts were sold mainly in stalls at state fairs. Shirts could be made to order with self-adhesive cloth letters or flocking, made popular by colleges and sports teams in the 1950s. Arturo Vega remembers making the first Ramones T-shirt at a fair in the Midwest, a white ringer T-shirt with red flocking letters. Vega had a unique relationship with the Ramones—he accompanied them on tour as the art director and would paint backdrops or handle lights. When the record company would not pay for him to fly with the band on their first tour to California in 1976, Vega decided to sell T-shirts to pay his way. At three dollars a pop, the screen-printed shirts flew out the door.

The iron-on transfer increased the availability of music T-shirts further. The process made it easy to mass-produce designs, and soon the winning combination of transfers and blank shirts were sold in every mall and shopping center. Perhaps the appeal, much like flocking at the fair or tie-dyeing in the kitchen sink, lay in the do-it-yourself nature of the process. This gave consumers the chance to make or customize their own T-shirt, a concept taken to extremes in England by Vivienne Westwood, Malcolm McLaren, and the Sex Pistols.

McLaren and Westwood ran a clothes store on Kings Road, which by 1975 was called Sex. They sold bondage gear made of rubber and leather as well as other countercultural products. When McLaren returned from a tour with the New York Dolls, he started making T-shirts influenced by the punk fashion of Richard Hell and the rest of New York's underground rock scene. Often printed inside out on the cheapest

5

T-shirts available, ripped, and then safety pinned, the T-shirts were a hit among young people with a taste for the subversive. One day John Lydon came into the store wearing a customized Pink Floyd T-shirt with the words "I Hate" scrawled on it in pen. McLaren was instantly impressed and asked Lydon to audition for a band he was putting together. Lydon became Johnny Rotten, and the Sex Pistols were born. McLaren merchandised and marketed the Sex Pistols heavily, combining the aesthetic of his shop with the economics and scale of modern rock promotion.

Musically, the 1980s were important for two reasons: the return of the superstar and the proliferation of the American underground. Madonna and Prince both broke down boundaries and became icons in the process. A young Michael Jackson became the King of Pop, selling more copies of his album *Thriller* than any other album in history. Meanwhile, bands such as Dead Kennedys and Black Flag began to release records and tour the world independently from the music industry. T-shirts enabled bands to expand their visual identity beyond record sleeves and concert posters. Fans could easily integrate a band's aesthetic into their own by wearing the T-shirt of their favorite artist

to school or a concert. For the underground band this meant an additional income to pay for gas or food. For the superstar, profits from merchandise skyrocketed from millions to billions. However, when the consumer excess of the 1980s reached a plateau, attitudes toward the band T-shirt shifted once again.

The Washington, D.C., band Fugazi, infamous for its strict ethical stance, refused to make any merchandise at all. In 1990 they even released a song called "Merchandise" ("You are not what you own"). But soon the ironic "This Is Not a Fugazi T-shirt" appeared on the market. The band did not want to make money selling their merchandise, but the bootleggers did.

In 1991 Nirvana seemingly came from nowhere to change mainstream music forever. The band embodied a new genre and encouraged fans to seek out their relatively obscure influences. In interviews Kurt Cobain consistently referenced the older bands that inspired him, from the Stooges to Sonic Youth. When Cobain wore a Daniel Johnston shirt to the MTV Video Music Awards and magazine photo shoots in 1992, the T-shirt generated so much interest that by the end of the year, independent artist Johnston was signed to Atlantic Records. By wearing the

T-shirt as a tribute and widening the success of one of his own favorite musicians, Cobain demonstrated the continuing cultural and commercial effect of the band T-shirt.

The evolution of the band T-shirt has been fast and furious. Various techniques and aesthetics have been employed over the years, the influence of which can be seen in contemporary examples in this book. Current bands and artists acknowledge the discourse of the band shirt with their own visual references. Throwback designs, ironic reworkings of iconic images, and even the trend of subtle, no-logo illustrations can be understood as a direct response to the designs that preceded it. But recently the art form has experienced a surge of popularity that has taken the band T-shirt to dizzying new heights.

Like the Band? Love the Shirt.

Does Paris Hilton really listen to the Ramones? Does she have a favorite Rolling Stones album? Probably not, but pick up any magazine and you'll see her wearing one of these bands' classic T-shirts anyway. The band T-shirt has become a phenomenon in its own right, just as much a fashion statement as a piece of music

memorabilia. But what does it mean when the T-shirt outsells the album, when the band's merchandise becomes more popular than the band itself?

Arturo Vega's appropriation of the presidential seal has become one of music's most iconic images: the Ramones logo. "It is satisfying to see the effectiveness of my work. . . . I believe in T-shirts as works of art. [They] are the single most important piece of popular culture. People want to identify with something." But he has mixed feelings about the popularity of the punk rock aesthetic.

Vega took his collection of Ramones memorabilia and official merchandise on the road for the 2006 Warped Tour. Stage clothes, backstage passes, original flyers, and some of the very first Ramones shirts were exhibited. "Kids would come up to me, mouths open— like, is this for real? But then they would say, 'I already have a Ramones shirt,' and walk away. . . . It's a shame; they only care about the shirts, not the music."

If, for some, wearing a classic band T-shirt is more about fashion than fandom, the appeal can be attributed to the current obsession for all things "vintage." In the past five years, cultural nostalgia has hit the collective consciousness—and it has hit hard. The intoxicating mix of nostalgia and irony has brought the vintage aesthetic to the forefront of mainstream street fashion. Lucrative licensing deals have led to the reissue of old designs on new shirts. No longer are they restricted to record stores and the back pages of rock magazines. The band T-shirt floats free in the sea of high- and low-fashion retail.

Saturation of the market with "retro" or "vintage-inspired" products has increased the value of more authentic pieces. T-shirts that not so long ago sat on the three-dollar rack at thrift stores now sell for seventy dollars at vintage boutiques. This demand for authenticity has led discerning consumers to the only place in the world where they can find anything in the world: eBay. It's like shooting rare fish in a barrel.

Fans and collectors have a love/hate relationship with the website that has a monopoly on all things old, rare, and otherwise hard to find. Although eBay may have taken the thrill out of the chase, unfortunately it has not cheapened it. Whether it's a hand-screened Hüsker Dü (New Alliance days) or mint condition Neil Young (circa *Rust Never Sleeps)*, be prepared to pay more than whatever you have in mind.

It may be a little disconcerting to see Jimi Hendrix shirts on a rack across from six packs of tube socks and discounted toasters, or a Bedazzled AC/DC shirt in the back-to-school range. But when you're looking at paying one hundred and fifty dollars to replace some shirt your mom used to mop the floor, the $9.95 range at Target starts to look surprisingly tasteful—especially if you're approaching thirty and still living with her.

The children of the baby boomers are doing whatever they can to stay younger longer. There has been a major shift in Western society toward what has been called an "extended adolescence," where today's young adults place the emphasis on the "young" over the "adult." In Britain the average age for children to leave their parents' home is twenty-eight. In the United States 65 percent of college graduates expect to live with their parents after graduation. The youth of today are living with their parents longer, studying longer, and delaying rites of passage such as career, marriage, and homeownership as long as seemingly possible. Oh, and they're dressing younger, too.

Ten to fifteen years ago young, urban professionals were wearing fine suits and cashmere.

Today's gainfully employed often arrive at the office in preworn jeans, limited-edition reissue sneakers, and their favorite Guns N' Roses T-shirt. And when they do have kids, they dress them in Misfits and Zeppelin, not Barney or Barbie.

If we choose clothes to represent ourselves to the rest of the world, what is it that we are trying to say? Metalheads in the office, punks in a limo, basement stoners with a baby stroller—the fact is that things just do not mean what they used to. Times change and images and their meanings change with them. And when meanings float free, when form is divorced from content, we can wear what we want and answer to no one.

"Dude, Metallica sucks!" "I know, but I like the shirt."

The band T-shirt is firmly entrenched in both music and fashion culture. It is with this in mind that we have put together this book. Rather than limiting ourselves to vintage (great band shirts have been made since 1989!), this book is a sampler of the band T-shirt in its various forms and genres. We believe it is possible to see the aesthetic wood for the fashion trees. And like so many others, we could not care less about Lindsay Lohan's new movie but love that circa 1975 John and Yoko shirt she's been wearing.

THE GREAT SOUTHERN COMPANY, 1975

Ira Sokoloff's road crew, selling five-dollar T-shirts for the Marshall Tucker Band at a Jimmy Carter benefit.

SHARA AND ADAM SOKOLOFF with family friend (left to right), 1973

Ira's daughter Shara is wearing the original Allman Brothers Band "Hell Yeah" shirt—the design was taken from an ad in the *Village Voice*.

IRA SOKOLOFF AND BUNKY ODOM, 1973

Ira with the assistant manager to the Allman Brothers Band, outside the Grand Opera House in Macon, Georgia. Ira is wearing the T-shirt he made for the Summer Jam at Watkins Glen.

1. Innovators

ELVIS PRESLEY
HEARTBREAK HOTEL

In 1956 Elvis's manager, Colonel Tom Parker, produced a number of souvenirs for fans to purchase. The book *Elvis Presley Memorabilia* by Sean O'Neal values this shirt today at approximately seven hundred dollars.

THE BEATLES
ABBEY ROAD

This is a rare promotional item from the Beatles' 1969 album *Abbey Road*. Apparently the band could not be bothered to have a proper photo shoot for the album cover, so they took this photo outside Abbey Road Studios.

From the collection of Jared Sagal

PAUL McCARTNEY & WINGS
LOGO

A well-worn Wings shirt, for the band McCartney formed with his first wife, Linda.
Note: sweat stains.

RINGO STARR
RINGO STARR

A portrait of the ever-smiling Ringo Starr, the former Beatle and narrator of kids' TV show *Thomas the Tank Engine*.

From the collection of Jared Sagal

THE ALLMAN BROTHERS BAND
MUSHROOM

This is the very first T-shirt the Allman Brothers produced. It was made for the band, crew, friends, and family in 1970.

From the collection of The Allman Brothers Band
The Allman Brothers Band logo courtesy The ABB Merchandising Co. Inc.

THE ALLMAN BROTHERS BAND
MUSHROOM

A multicolor version of the original Mushroom design by Wonder Graphics Inc., from 1973.

From the collection of The Allman Brothers Band
The Allman Brothers Band logo courtesy The ABB Merchandising Co. Inc.

THE ALLMAN BROTHERS BAND

In 1973 the Allman Brothers Band and merchandiser Ira Sokoloff collaborated with local promoters to produce event shirts for individual shows. This particular shirt was made to commemorate the naming of the venue in memory of Duane Allman.

21

From the collection of The Allman Brothers Band
The Allman Brothers Band logo courtesy The ABB Merchandising Co. Inc.

THE ALLMAN BROTHERS BAND
ENLIGHTENED ROGUES

A great copper-ink print from the Allman Brothers' 1979 tour for their album *Enlightened Rogues.*

From the collection of Jared Sagal

THE GRATEFUL DEAD
SKULL & ROSES

This design initially appeared on the cover of *Grateful Dead,* the double live album released in 1971 also known as *Skull & Roses* and *Skullfuck* (the title originally pitched to and rejected by the record company). Cult collaborators Alton Kelley and Stanley Mouse designed the album cover. The

black-and-white illustration of the skeleton was taken from a nineteenth-century edition of the Rubáiyát of Omar Khayyám.

From the collection of Courtney Shanks

THE GRATEFUL DEAD
NEW YEAR'S EVE 1989

When a psychedelic jester is dancing with a skeleton, you know it's New Year's Eve and you know the Grateful Dead are playing.

From the collection of Brad Shanks

YES
BOOTLEG

27

A bastardized version of a Roger Dean design.

YES
TALES FROM TOPOGRAPHIC OCEANS

This shirt was made in tribute to one created for the international Tales tour, which began in England in 1973 and continued in the United States in 1974.

"We made almost every mistake
you could think of: We put our emphasis on posters and other paper products and started with only one shirt design and that in a range of sizes that were on average a couple of sizes too small; we imported the shirts into England, printed them, and then shipped them to the U.S.A., sometimes shipping product every other day. However, we gradually learnt and by the end of the tour we were getting it right. Mick Warwood and his partner, who were responsible for the day-to-day organization, became the basis for Brockum International, which in turn became a four-hundred-million-dollar-a-year company.

"The band Yes strongly supported the idea of controlling the quality, which made it possible, and when we made a clear profit of about $250,000 we were astounded and very relieved.

"Over the years, however, controlling quality has always been an issue."

—Roger Dean

YES
RELAYER

This shirt is a reprint of a design originally used for the tour in 1975.

BOB DYLAN
U.S. TOUR '78

How cute is this shirt? From Bob Dylan's 1978 tour for his album *Street Legal.*

From the collection of Jared Sagal

THE ROLLING STONES
LIPS '81

"On 29 April 1970, Jo Bergman, who was running the Stones' office at the time, wrote to me to confirm that they had commissioned me to design a poster for their forthcoming 1970 European tour. At this time I was in my final year of a graduate design course at the Royal College of Art in London. I was very honored when Mick Jagger turned up at the college to see my final degree show.

"A short time later I met with Mick again, who asked me to design a logo or symbol for the Rolling Stones' record label. Mick showed me an image of the Goddess of Kali, which was the starting point to our discussion regarding the design of the logo. A great interest of mine at the time was pop art and would have been an inspiration and it took several rough drafts to hone the design into an entity which I felt worked. I was paid fifty pounds for the design, which took me about a week to complete. In 1972 I was paid an additional two hundred pounds in recognition of the logo's success.

"The first use of the logo was the inner sleeve for the *Sticky*

Fingers album. The outer sleeve was designed by Warhol, hence the mix-up with the credits. The logo was not fully registered in all countries, and a German jeans company registered the logo in Germany for their own products. This situation, and the fact that the tongue was getting used by unauthorized manufacturers of badges and T-shirts, prompted proper registration and a merchandising agreement with myself to capitalize on the success of the logo.

"The design concept for the tongue was to represent the band's anti-authoritarian attitude, Mick's mouth, and the obvious sexual connotations. I designed it in such a way that it was easily reproduced and in a style which I thought could stand the test of time. Due to its immediate popularity, the Stones kept with it over the years and I believe that it represents one of the strongest and most recognizable logos worldwide. And of course I'm proud of that. The simplicity of the design lent itself to many variations, which were done by other designers and not myself. The Stones ultimately bought the copyright but I still own the hand-drawn artwork."

—John Pasche

THE ROLLING STONES
LIPS '81

THE ROLLING STONES
LIPS '89

Spot the differences.

From the collection of Abby Klein

THE ROLLING STONES
DRAGON '81

A baseball shirt from the Rolling Stones' tour for *Tattoo You* in 1981. At the time it was the biggest tour the band had done.

THE ROLLING STONES
STEEL WHEELS

After a couple of years of downtime and solo albums, Keith Richards and Mick Jagger reunited in 1989 for the Rolling Stones' album *Steel Wheels*.

From the collection of Courtney Shanks

LED ZEPPELIN
SWAN SONG

Led Zeppelin launched their record label Swan Song (named after their unreleased ditty) when their contract with Atlantic Records expired in late 1973. The label's logo, based on the painting *Evening: Fall of Day* by William Rimmer (1869), has become a classic T-shirt design. An original, and well-loved, example is shown above.

Led Zeppelin photos courtesy of MYTHGEM

From the collection of Jared Sagal

39

UNITED STATES OF
AMERICA 1977

LED ZEPPELIN

II

This shirt depicts the cover of Led Zeppelin's album *Led Zeppelin II*. The cover was designed by David Juniper based on a photograph of the Jasta Division of the German air force of World War One, with the faces of the band members airbrushed onto the heads of four of the pilots.

LED ZEPPELIN
STAIRWAY

The painting on this shirt, from their 1971 album *Led Zeppelin IV*, has become synonymous with the song "Stairway to Heaven." The symbols on the back were picked by each band member: The first was designed by Jimmy Page and its meaning has since been forgotten; the second, chosen by John Paul Jones, represents a person with confidence and competence; the third, chosen by John Bonham,

represents the religious idea of the trio or of threes; and the fourth, chosen by Robert Plant, is a feather of truth and justice, enclosed within the unbroken circle of eternal life.

Led Zeppelin photos courtesy of MYTHGEM
From the collection of Jared Sagal

EMERSON, LAKE & PALMER
IRON-ON

This T-shirt is a classic example of the 1970s D.I.Y. phenomenon: the iron-on.

From the collection of Pam and Dave Leto

JAMES BROWN
PLEASE! PLEASE! PLEASE!

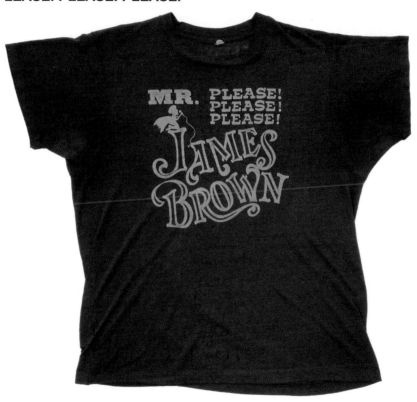

Among other titles such as the Godfather of Soul, the Hardest-Working Man in Show Business, and Soul Brother Number One, James Brown is also often referred to as Mr. Please, Please, Please, after his first single, 1959's "Please, Please, Please."

From the collection of Dave Buick

MARTHA AND THE VANDELLAS

"While I'd love to be able to say I got a Bo Diddley shirt from when I saw him in '72, or an Isley Brothers' shirt from when I saw them in '76, the truth is we didn't have a lot of money in those days, and no one in my family was going to pay a lot of money for a shirt I wasn't going to fit in six months later. I bought my first shirt with my own money, probably in 1983, and believe it or not, it was Martha and the Vandellas. A local punk fashion store had a brief line of bootleg Motown artist shirts; I never made it back to get any of the others. I still have the shirt."

—Mick Collins, The Dirtbombs/The Gories

RICK JAMES
STREET SONGS

This baseball T-shirt from 1981 features the artwork from Rick James's album that year, *Street Songs*. Mostly made up of songs dealing with prostitution and life on the streets, the album features Rick's biggest hit, "Super Freak."

From the collection of Abby Klein

WILD CHERRY

Play that funky music, white boy.

From the collection of Abby Klein

RUSH
SIGNALS

"The artwork for every Rush album except the first two have been designed by Hugh Syme. As Rush's music is somewhat technical and different, the artwork follows suit. Album jackets such as *Hemispheres*, *Permanent Waves*, and *Signals* (featured on this shirt) are good examples of that. There is a lot of subtle humor used in the artwork, and this follows the demeanor of the band."

—Patrick McLoughlin, Rush merchandiser

QUEEN
TOUR '80

From Queen's 1980 tour in support of their album *The Game*, which includes the smash hit "Another One Bites the Dust."

Appears courtesy of Queen Productions Ltd.
From the collection of Abby Klein

QUEEN
AMERICAN TOUR 1982

A Queen baseball T-shirt from the U.S. tour in 1982.

53

JEFFERSON STARSHIP
MODERN TIMES

A baseball T-shirt from their 1981 tour for the album *Modern Times*.

From the collection of Catie Donhauser

KING CRIMSON
DISCIPLINE

From their 1981 album *Discipline*.

DEEP PURPLE
PERFECT STRANGERS

From their 1984 album *Perfect Strangers*.

THE DOOBIE BROTHERS
EAGLE

The Doobie Brothers were originally called Pud.

PETER FRAMPTON
NUMERO UNO

A nice portrait of teen-star-turned-guitar-god Peter Frampton.

TED NUGENT
TOUR '78

The NRA's most famous rocker is Ted Nugent, aiming that guitar/bow at a deer/hog on this tour shirt from 1978.

63

JOURNEY
FRONTIERS

This baseball T-shirt is from Journey's 1983 world tour in support of their album *Frontiers.*

65

OZZY OSBOURNE
BARK AT THE MOON

A baseball T-shirt from Ozzy's 1984 tour in support of his album *Bark at the Moon*.

JUDAS PRIEST
PAINKILLER

The Painkiller is a fictional character from the Judas Priest album of the same name. Here he is seen riding his motorcycle, which is part dragon and has circular saws for wheels. This shirt was originally used during the band's 1990–91 tour with Megadeth and Testament.

From the collection of Pam and Dave Leto

2. New Genres

RAMONES
SIRE

This is the first Ramones shirt to be made for the band by their record company Sire. It was made in 1976 to promote their debut album, *The Ramones*.

Designer Arturo Vega was already working on eagle images when he went to Washington, D.C., with the Ramones. "We saw the logos and flags of all the government agencies, but when we went to the White House, I saw the presidential seal and was like, 'Bingo!'"

From the collection of Arturo Vega

RAMONES
ROCKET TO RUSSIA

Another great presidential design from Arturo Vega. Vega was at odds with the cartoonish way the band was often represented and was keen to represent the band in a more serious manner.

From the collection of Arturo Vega

THE CLASH
STRAIGHT TO HELL

"Straight to Hell" is a song from the Clash's 1982 album *Combat Rock*. The song is about the Amerasian blues—the abandonment of the illegitimate children of American soldiers during the Vietnam War.

From the collection of Jared Sagal

TALKING HEADS
TANK

This bootleg singlet sports a Talking Heads logo inspired by the Honshu Tigers. It was sold outside a concert on their 1983 U.S. tour.

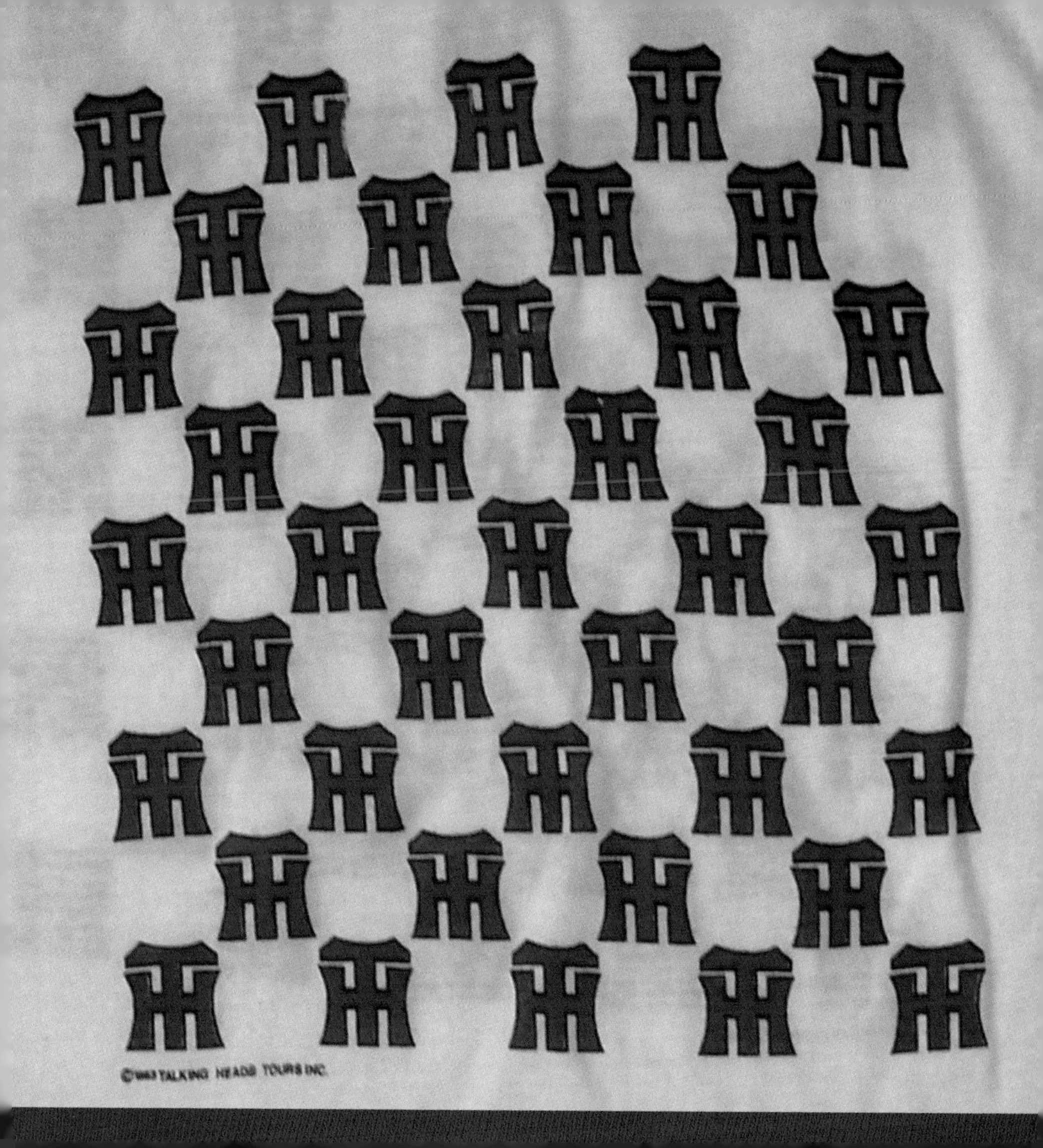
TALKING HEADS TOURS INC.

SEX PISTOLS
NEVER MIND THE BOLLOCKS

This rare gem was a Warner Brothers promotional item used for the U.S. release of the Sex Pistols' only studio album, *Never Mind the Bollocks, Here's the Sex Pistols.* Design by Jamie Reid.

JOY DIVISION
UNKNOWN PLEASURES

This popular Joy Division shirt is a version of the cover of their 1979 debut album, *Unknown Pleasures*. Designed by Peter Saville, the picture represents one hundred pulses from the first pulsar discovered in 1967. The image remains one of the most recognizable symbols in music today.

From the collection of Michael Nagin

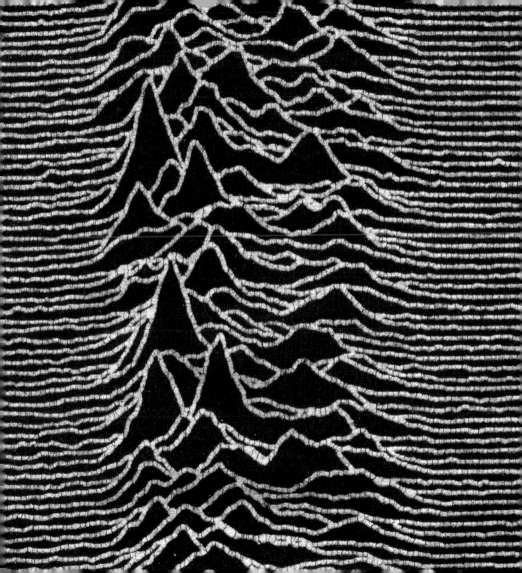

NEW ORDER
CEREMONY

This T-shirt design is from the cover of New Order's 1981 single "Ceremony" (FAC. 33). It was designed by Factory Records' in-house artists Peter Saville and Brett Wickens. It is an appropriation of the Albertus type specimen created by Berthold Wolpe in 1937. An American company, Object Merchandise, manufactured this particular shirt.

"If every merchandiser produced
work like this, designers would be proud to see their work.
The bronze ink looks like it's sitting there like metal on a shirt."

—Peter Saville

IGGY POP
1980

This rare wonder is from Iggy's nightclubbing tour of 1980. The song "Nightclubbing" was co-written by David Bowie during their furtive cohabitation in Berlin in the late 1970s.

**nightclubbing
1980**

688 CLUB *atlanta*

BOOKIE'S *detroit*

WAVES *chicago*

B'GINNINGS *schaumberg*

MERLINS *madison*

83

MISFITS
SKULL

One of punk rock's most famous images, the Misfits' logo was actually taken from a serialized television show, *The Crimson Ghost,* from 1946. This, paired with a typeface appropriated from the magazine *Famous Monsters of Filmland,* created one of the most enduring band aesthetics in rock history.

From the collection of Aimee Egdell

BLACK FLAG
NERVOUS BREAKDOWN

The cover of Black Flag's first single, "Nervous Breakdown," is a drawing by Greg Ginn's brother, Raymond Pettibon. It was the first release of Ginn's SST Records, a label that would blaze trails in American underground music.

From Artie Phillie's pile of dirty clothes

DEAD KENNEDYS
DK

"I'd been playing around with it for a while, drawing out chicken scratches; I wanted to make sure it was something simple and easy to spray-paint so people would graffiti it all over the place. And then I showed it to Winston Smith, he played around with it, came back with a bunch of designs that had the circle and slightly 3-D-looking letters, and he had ones with different patterns behind it. I liked the one with bricks, but ultimately I thought simple red behind it was the boldest and the best.

"Winston Smith was a rabble-rousing guerilla artist who's mainly known for his collages now. He could also draw really well. A woman I knew gave him my address and said we should meet. So I get this postcard in the mail with a still from the Zapruder film where Kennedy's brain is exploding. 'If you want more, write me back, Winston Smith.' So I wrote him back and then he sent me this big package of collages, a self-portrait which is him with a gas mask on, standing in the middle of a military graveyard. He sent me fake credit cards with names like Vice and Masterscam, some kind of scary-ass fake detergent he enclosed, Radioactive Detergent, and some other things. Then I wrote him back again and asked for a phone number and we've been inseparable ever since."

—Jello Biafra, Dead Kennedys

"The Minor Threat shirt design was originally used

on fifty Minor Threat 'Out of Step' 12" EP test pressings, and then I decided it would make a nice T-shirt. The black sheep was taken from the artwork Cynthia Connolly had done for 'Out of Step,' which featured one black sheep running away from a flock of white sheep. The type used for Minor Threat was blown up from several different typefaces we'd had done late at night at the *Washington Post*, when our singer, Ian's, dad still worked there.

"I remember screening the black sheep on several things other than T-shirts, including a skateboard ramp, on Ian's skateboard, and on the side of the red van owned by our friends in the band Scream. It was fairly common for bands to carry their T-shirt screens with them when they went on tour so they could screen shirts when they ran out. The Big Boys (from Texas) screened their stuff on our shirts and pillowcases. I remember Social Distortion and Youth Brigade (both bands from California) were visiting the Dischord house. One guy traveling with them needed to wash out his screens after printing some shirts, and we didn't yet have a hose. He went across the street to try to borrow one from a neighbor, not realizing that Helen Halderman was our archenemy. She was quite heavy and had a short haircut, and when he asked, 'Excuse me, sir, do you have a hose I could borrow?' it did not exactly endear us further with her (we later became great friends, once we got to know each other). Our guitarist, Lyle, also had some shirts and sweatshirts printed with the whole flock of sheep and the Minor Threat logo, which we sold on tour. Ian was not terribly in favor of selling merchandise, but he let the band be a democracy, and we certainly needed what little money the shirts brought us."

—Jeff Nelson, Minor Threat/Dischord Records

DISCHORD
D.C. HARDCORE

"I designed this Dischord shirt in 1981 for the small record company I run with Ian MacKaye. The design consists of the logo I created above a photograph taken by our friend Susie Josephson. At the time I was crazy about a great Australian band, the Saints, and the logo very much reflects that. The photo was taken at a Minor Threat show at Wilson Center in Washington, D.C., and shows Ian surrounded by friends, all singing along. I had to flip the picture horizontally to make it all fit with the logo, so now when we look at the real picture it looks wrong somehow.

"Blank T-shirts came in really boring colors back then, and I chose to do the Dischord shirts on tan, red, and on special-order heather-gray athletic shirts. Eventually all I used were the heather-gray shirts. I printed them in the leaky garage of our group house on a homemade printer and sold them at shows and through the mail. I got grief from some quarters for selling them for the outlandish price of seven dollars postpaid. (The blank shirt cost about four dollars, postage one dollar, and the envelope twenty-five cents!) Many in the punk scene felt it was wrong to profit from anything, and from early on there was a strongly felt admonition not to 'sell out.' To me it is fascinating how the dichotomy still exists and has become even more stark in the punk scene, with record (and merchandise) sales unimaginable twenty-five years ago still bringing cries of 'sell-out!'

"It may sound strange, but T-shirts were an example of why Ian and I stopped playing in bands together by 1986. I thought they were perfectly acceptable accompaniments to our music, and products I took pride in making. Growing up as a kid, I was always forming little companies with my brothers, and naming the companies and creating their logos was paramount in fun and importance. For me, creating products to sell and marketing them was exciting. Ian, on the other hand, came to view T-shirts and other 'tie-ins' as distractions from the music, as vocalized in his later band Fugazi's song 'Merchandise.' We decided it was better to stay friends and keep the record label going instead of butting heads over something like T-shirts. Therefore, Dischord itself sold no T-shirts after about 1982, and I sold them myself."

—Jeff Nelson, Minor Threat/Dischord Records

"The 'joyride' T-shirt was designed by G.I.'s longtime T-shirt guy, Andy Armstrong, a.k.a. T-shirt Andy. Andy was a rail-thin young man who sported a tall double-mohawk and always wore his leather jacket. Those multicolored liberty spikes of his were some kind of impressive! He may have looked scary or mean to an outsider, but to people who knew him, Andy was a pussycat of a punk. Out of all the Government Issue designs, the "joyride" T-shirt was the most popular.

"And what became of Andy? He's now a big gore-meister horror movie–shirt and doll (he's big into Joey Ramone, Manson, and Dahmer . . . eeek!) designer who goes under the name Andrew T. Gore."

—John Stab, Government Issue

GOVERNMENT ISSUE

From the collection of Dorien Garry

DAG NASTY

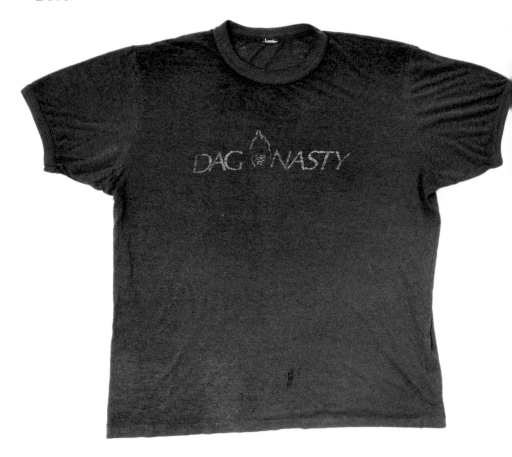

Can I Say this is an awesome shirt?

95

NEGATIVE APPROACH
TIED DOWN

This shirt, featuring the cover of Negative Approach's only album, *Tied Down,* was originally owned by their singer, John Brannon.

From the collection of Dave Buick

PUBLIC ENEMY
BASEBALL

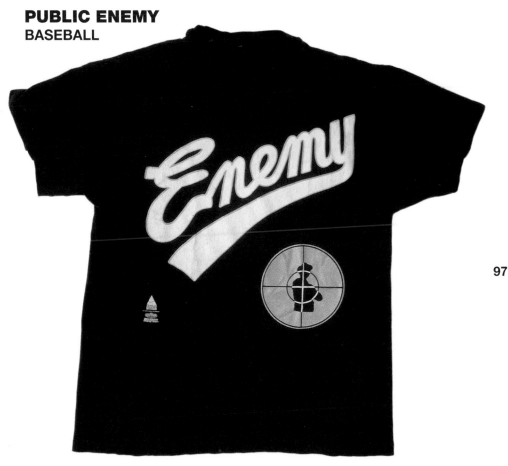

The classic Public Enemy logo of the man in the gun sights was hand-drawn by Chuck D himself, and the man in the sights is said to be fellow rapper E Love.

From the collection of Abby Klein

PUBLIC ENEMY
FEAR OF A BLACK PLANET

From their 1990 album *Fear of a Black Planet*.

From the collection of Sean Nagin

PUBLIC ENEMY
IT TAKES A NATION OF MILLIONS TO HOLD US BACK

This is a 1988 shirt for their album *It Takes a Nation of Millions to Hold Us Back*. The red and blue coloring on the stars and stripes is the crowning jewel.

RUN DMC
RAISING HELL

From their 1986 album *Raising Hell*.

103

RUN DMC
TOUGHER THAN LEATHER

From their 1988 album *Tougher Than Leather.*

AFRIKA BAMBAATAA
RENEGADES OF FUNK

Taken from the cover of his third record, 1983's *Renegades of Funk.*

From the collection of Dave Buick

ALICE COOPER
THE NIGHTMARE RETURNS

This shirt is from Alice Cooper's 1986 tour for his album *The Nightmare Returns.* Staged beheadings, as depicted here, were common at Alice Cooper concerts of the time.

Courtesy of Nightmare Inc. • From the collection of the authors

MOTÖRHEAD
10TH ANNIVERSARY

Motörhead's Warpig (affectionately known as Snaggletooth B. Motörhead) was designed by Joe Petagno for the cover of their self-titled debut album and is one of the most iconic logos in rock. This example, made for the band's tenth anniversary in 1985, is backed by the spade symbol referring to the band's most famous song, "Ace of Spades."

109

MOTÖRHEAD
WARPIG

"Lemmy always said if as many people bought their albums who wore Motörhead T-shirts, they'd be rich. That is pretty classic, the iron mask, a good design. Once a band gets that, you know, something like the Ramones logo, you can just keep selling it."

—Dale Crover, The Melvins

SCORPIONS
BLACKOUT

The cover off their 1982 album, featuring a self-portrait from Austrian artist Gottfried Helnwein.

113

SCORPIONS
TOUR '84

A bikinied Viking shirt from the Scorpions' 1984 tour for their album *Love at First Sting*. The album became a huge hit with its first single, "Rock You Like a Hurricane." The song has been featured on *The Simpsons*, *Little Nicky*, and *Jawbreaker*, and plays before every Carolina Hurricanes ice hockey game.

115

METALLICA
. . . AND JUSTICE FOR ALL

This 1988 Metallica shirt is made for the band's fourth album, . . . *And Justice for All*. This is the first shirt to feature new bassist Jason Newsted after the death of bassist Cliff Burton in 1986.

From the collection of Abby Klein

IRON MAIDEN
NEWSPRINT

Eddie the Head is the name of Iron Maiden's mascot. Frequently featured in artwork and live shows, Eddie was originally drawn by Derek Riggs based on a mask that featured on the band's first album and early concerts. Here, Eddie takes on The Man against the backdrop of a great newsprint shirt.

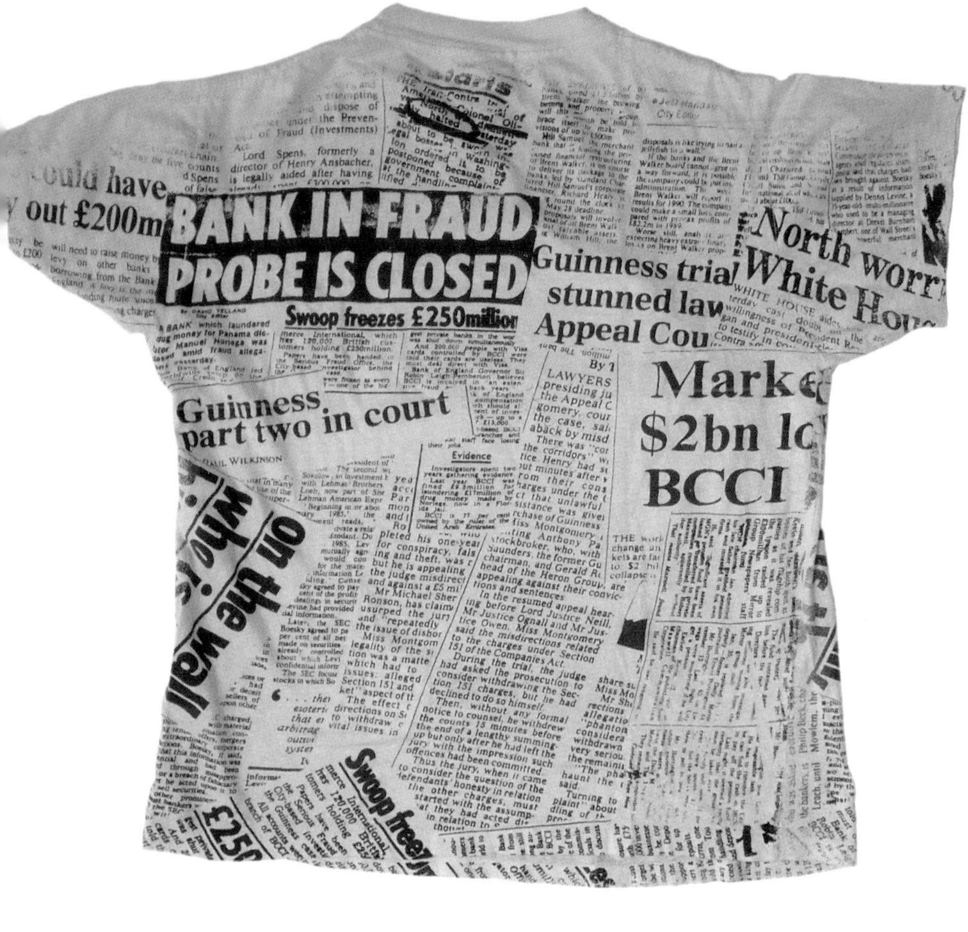

From the collection of Jared Sagal

PANTERA
DOMINATION

Perfect for Halloween, this Pantera shirt even glows in the dark!

121

SLAYER
DECADE OF AGGRESSION

Decade of Aggression is the live double album that Slayer released in 1991. The imperialist logo with the eagle and swords had been used since 1990's *Seasons in the Abyss*.

123

SLAYER
SLAYTANIC WEHRMACHT

Another militaristic T-shirt from Slayer. Slaytanic Wehrmacht is the name of the band's fan club.

ROY ORBISON
THE LEGEND

In 1963, Roy Orbison headlined a European tour with the Beatles. At one show Orbison, who had poor vision, left his glasses in an airplane, so he wore his prescription sunglasses onstage instead. The look was a hit so he wore those sunglasses for not only the rest of the tour but also the rest of his career. This shirt is from the 1980s.

From the collection of Dave Buick

WILLIE NELSON

One of the proudest Texans in music, this country superstar celebrates his home-state pride on this 1984 ringer.

From the collection of Sameena Ahmad

HANK WILLIAMS, JR.
BOCEPHUS

Hank Williams, Jr., got his nickname from his father, who thought that as a baby he looked like a television ventriloquist dummy named Bocephus.

129

BRUCE SPRINGSTEEN
GOD CREATED

Say no more.

BRUCE SPRINGSTEEN
IRON-ON

Back in the 1970s you could just pick a design at the store and put it on your favorite shirt with your mom's iron.

From the collection of Abby Klein

BRUCE SPRINGSTEEN
WORLD TOUR

This baseball T-shirt from the Boss's tour of 1980–81 features a drawing of the cover of his 1975 album *Born to Run*.

BRUCE SPRINGSTEEN
AND THE E STREET BAND
1980-81 WORLD TOUR
USA
SPAIN
FRANCE
NORWAY
GERMANY
UNITED KINGDOM
THE NETHERLANDS
SWITZERLAND
DENMARK
SWEDEN
BELGIUM
CANADA

133

From the collection of Jane Liddle

MADONNA
EROTICA

Madonna established herself as a pop icon in the 1980s. This T-shirt at the time of her album *Erotica* is an obvious play on that status.

From her 1993 tour, The Girlie Show, which was inspired by an Edward Hopper painting of a burlesque dancer.

This shirt was designed to celebrate Squeeze's arrival in the United States on June 15, 1982, at Kennedy Airport.

137

THE CURE

This shirt is from 1985, circa the album *The Head on the Door*. The artwork originally appeared on the single for *In Between Days* from that same album.

MORRISSEY
PORTRAIT

While the Smiths' aesthetic focused on images of celebrity and stardom, a successful solo career kept Morrissey in the center of the frame. Here is a great snapshot from the beginning of his solo career in the late 1980s.

From the collection of Arty Sheperd

HAPPY MONDAYS

This design was originally used in 1988 for the Happy Mondays single *Wrote for Luck,* was later used on the inside cover for their album *Bummed* from the same year, and was used as a tour T-shirt to promote both. This bright and bold shirt, with its wink to '60s hippie culture, is typical of the "Madchester" scene and the beginning of the rave aesthetic.

3. We Heart the '90s

RIDE
GOING BLANK AGAIN

The cover of their second album, 1992's *Going Blank Again*.

143

"We were going through
a Beatles *White Album* phase (Revolution No. 9)
and had a couple of versions of a song called
'Opportunity' (from the first album, *Some Friendly*)
version 3 and version 9, so I guess the shirt comes
from that. . . . And also we loved Factory Records,
who used to number everything they did . . .
records, T-shirts, the factory cat, etc."

—Tim Burgess, The Charlatans

THE CHARLATANS
VIVA LA SOCIALE

"'Vive la Sociale' is a song by the Charlatans and it reminded me of the Sid Vicious/Vivienne Westwood shirt Viva la Rock. We just stole the idea."

—Tim Burgess, The Charlatans

From the collection of Michael Nagin

Brian Cannon, who also designed the artwork for the group's first three albums, created this Oasis logo.

From the collection of Arty Sheperd

BLUR
MODERN LIFE IS RUBBISH

This shirt was made in 1993 on the occasion of a U.K. tour to celebrate the release of Blur's second album, *Modern Life Is Rubbish* (originally called *Blur vs America*). The T-shirt features the album cover, a painting by Paul Gribble.

149

PRIMAL SCREAM
MTHR FCKR

Primal Scream's MTHR FCKR T-shirt was made for the tour for their 2000 album *XTRMNTR*, although it embodies the angst of the 1990s English music scene quite nicely.

From the collection of Carlos Ladino

PIXIES
DEATH TO THE PIXIES

This shirt was made in the early 1990s. The band broke up soon after, and the phrase was used as the title of their greatest-hits album.

From the collection of Justin Tripp

VIOLENT FEMMES
VIOLENT FEMMES

The Violent Femmes' self-titled debut album went Platinum ten years after it was released in 1982.

From the collection of Jared Sagal

LUNA

Another great design from Tannis Root.

THIS IS NOT A FUGAZI T-SHIRT

"In the mid-1980s, it seemed to me that there was an enormous emphasis on selling merchandise at shows. This was really the beginning of what has now become something akin to a rolling shopping mall at many gigs.

"When Fugazi first went out on tour, in 1987, we were really struck by the demand for T-shirts coming from the kids at the shows. People would ask us if we had shirts while we were still loading in, and when we said no, they seemed almost offended. Fugazi didn't have a record out, and we had never played their town, so they hadn't even heard our music, but still they wanted to buy shirts. The fact we didn't sell anything seemed almost blasphemous! Their reaction confirmed that we were on to something good.

"Fuck making shirts!

"Of course, our decision made it even easier for bootleggers to print up and sell shirts and stickers. Bear in mind that they would have done it even if we were in the game, but we figured that at least this way it clearly illuminated the greed that exists in that strange parallel economy of music. In the beginning, it was mostly small companies, and they would knock it off if I called them. They usually offered to pay us, sort of a 'retro-licensing' deal, but the answer was no, as that would have been our position from the beginning.

"I managed to trace one design back to a fairly well-known T-shirt company in the Boston area, and I called to tell them to cut it out. I spoke to the main guy there, and, of course, he wanted to do a deal. And, of course, the answer was no. Still, we had a nice chat. He was curious why we didn't want to sell shirts, and after I explained our position, he seemed to respect it. About one month later, a friend at a record store alerted me to the 'This is not a Fugazi T-shirt' shirt. I traced it back to the same Boston dude. What a smart motherfucker he was! I called him up and said, 'Okay, you're funny and you're creative, so let's see how creative you are with the accounting.' I asked him to choose an organization doing good work in his community and give them what would amount to the band's royalty for the shirts. I think he chose a women's shelter up there, and as far as I know he sent them money right up until he quit the business."

—Ian MacKaye, Fugazi

From the collection of Jeff Nelson

FAITH NO MORE
LANGUAGE

This Faith No More shirt shows the band's name in seven different languages on the back—a multi-cultural classic!

157

Another Faith No More shirt with their classic Star of David design. This shirt was sold on their The Real Thing tour in 1989.

159

© Faith No More
From the collection of Sean Nagin

SWANS
GREED

Okay, so this one is actually from 1985, but they were ahead of their time.

THE GORIES
BLACK CAT

"Printed in limited quantities and sold mostly on their implosive 1992 European tour, the Gories' only T-shirt 'borrows' its design from a box of Black Cat candles. This specific specimen was found in a Detroit thrift store and was obtained via trade for a Greenhornes 45. Long considered a status symbol amongst hipster elite, they can usually be found draped across blasé used-record store clerks or underneath a Brooks leather jacket in the middle of a smoky Cass Corridor dive bar." —Ben Blackwell, The Dirtbombs

From the collection of Ben Blackwell

95 SOUTH
WHOOT, THERE IT IS

"Excuse me, Sonny. You know where I could find some booty?" So started this one-hit wonder from 1993. Ideal for spring break, this T-shirt sums up the song perfectly.

163

SONIC YOUTH/FIREHOSE

This shirt was made for the Sonic Youth and fIREHOSE's Flaming Telepaths U.S. tour in fall 1986. Each flame represents a stop on the tour, and on the bottom left there is a list of the birthplaces of each member of both bands. T-shirt designed by fIREHOSE guitarist Ed Crawford.

SONIC YOUTH
GOO

In 1990 Sonic Youth released their eighth full-length album. The front cover features a Raymond Pettibon drawing, with the iconic caption "I stole my sister's boyfriend. It was all whirlwind, heat, and flash. Within a week we killed my parents and hit the road." This design typically appears on a plain white or black T-shirt, making this yellow tie-dyed version even sweeter.

From the collection of Justin Tripp

SONIC YOUTH
DIRTY

This baseball T-shirt comes from Sonic Youth's 1992 album *Dirty*. The cover was designed by Mike Kelley and features a series of cute but sinister soft toys. The "Gracias" on the back has become as iconic as the bunny on the front.

167

SONIC YOUTH
POP

A tour T-shirt from the Dirty tour of 1992, with a sweet picture of Saturn on the back.

169

SONIC YOUTH
ASTRONAUGHT

Colorful, adventurous, and intergalactic, with floral notes.

DINOSAUR JR
COW

This classic "grunge" shirt, often worn by members of Nirvana in photo shoots and media appearances, is based on a soft toy that Jay Mascis owned as a child.

From the collection of Alexis Brooks

BOREDOMS
INDEX

This T-shirt from Japan's favorite psych-kraut-punk band Boredoms features a back print with diagrams displaying every shirt they made up until that point. This T-shirt appears in its own index as number 19.

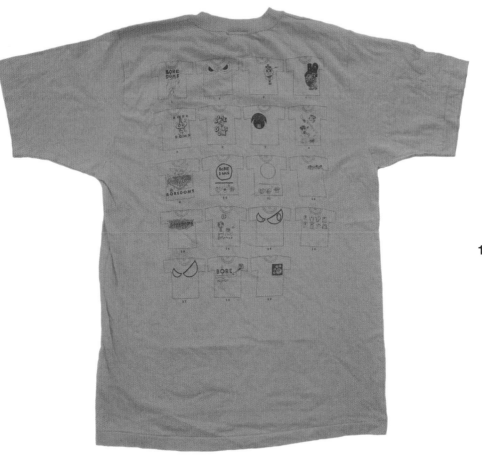

From the Tannis Root archives

SHELLAC
OMO

Clear ink on a black T-shirt—with wear and tear the shirt will fade and the logo, protected by the ink, will become more apparent. The OMO design is the logo of the Russian company Lomo, which make microscopes, cameras, and microphones that Shellac often uses for its recordings. Shellac's use of the design dates back to its first release.

175

REDD KROSS
NEUROTICA

"We first met Tannis Root on our first tour in '84. Madonna had taken naked pictures before she was Madonna and in '84 or '85 *Penthouse* ran them. We were on tour looking for that issue of *Penthouse*; there was a lot of anticipation building up to that issue being on the stands. When we were in Raleigh we met our now-longtime friends Bill Mooney and Barbara Herring. They not only had the issue, but they'd

already made silk screens. So we stayed with them that night, stayed up all night, and ran our own nude Madonna T-shirts. And to my recollection those were the first Tannis Root shirts."

—Steve McDonald, Redd Kross

From the Tannis Root archives

MUDHONEY
THE JOY OF GOING DOWN

"The Happy Flaming Airplane illustration (circa 1991), also known as The Joy of Going Down, by Edwin Judah Fotheringham from Mudhoney's *Every Good Boy Deserves Fudge* album, is a clear indication of the artist's pre–9/11 mindset."

—Mark Arm, Mudhoney

From the collection of Pete Ciccotto

Mudhoney

every good boy deserves fudge.

MUDHONEY
SOFT HELL

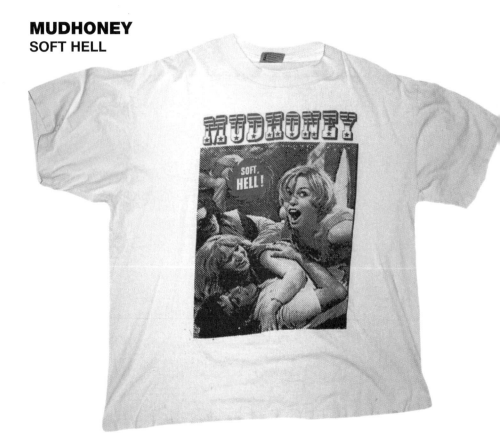

"Soft Hell! Hell yeah, that's a great shirt!"
—Mark Arm, Mudhoney

MELVINS
ARMY

"We probably first did them in the early '90s. . . . Even Gene Simmons saw one; he said, 'Gimme one of those and I'll wear it all over the place,' and next thing we know he's on the cover of *Metal Hammer* magazine wearing it. He said he realized the T-shirt was a tribute, but that when people are blatantly trying to rip KISS off is when they send their lawyers after them." —Dale Crover, Melvins

From the collection of Pete Ciccotto

MELVINS
FIEND CLUB

Another in the Melvins' series of tribute T-shirts, this time an appropriation of the famous Misfits logo, which itself is an appropriation.

NIRVANA
INCESTICIDE

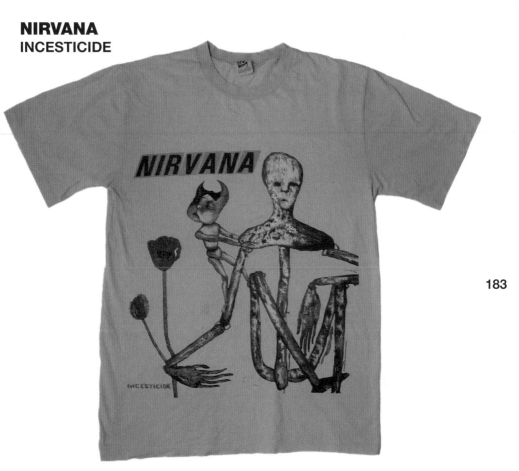

This is the first band T-shirt that Henry (co-author) ever owned. The picture is the cover of their 1992 B-sides and rarities album, *Incesticide,* and is a painting by Kurt Cobain.

From the collection of the authors

NIRVANA
HEART-SHAPED BOX

This great all-over print shirt was taken from the cover of the single "Heart-Shaped Box" from Nirvana's 1993 album *In Utero*.

185

HELMET

This Helmet T-shirt from 1990 features the cover of their EP from that same year, *Born Annoying*.

RED HOT CHILI PEPPERS

Red Hot Chili Peppers at their fluorescent best.

Sarah Utter, the guitarist and singer in Bangs, designed this shirt.

JAWBREAKER
WHEN IT PAINS IT ROARS

189

"I gave this shirt to Kurt Cobain when we toured with Nirvana in 1993. It now hangs in the window at Guitar Center in Hollywood." —Adam Pfahler, Jawbreaker

Design by Adam Pfahler.

From the collection of Franco Castiglioni

JONATHAN FIRE*EATER

"This T-shirt was purchased from the band at their October 1998 show at the Shelter in Detroit. The merch special offered that night was a shirt, a full-length CD, and a 7-inch single, all for the low, low price of five dollars. Apparently some of these shirts had become stained with human blood and thus were bleached before they were sold, quite possibly the earliest example of the 'pre-worn' phenomenon. The stain on this particular shirt can still be faintly made out approximately two inches to the left of '1998,' and it looks like there was a lot of blood."

—Ben Blackwell, The Dirtbombs

BECK

Hand-screened by the man himself on a thrift-store T-shirt.

193

From the collection of Vicki Farrell

FLAMING LIPS
ALIEN

When the Flaming Lips were signed to Warner Brothers in 1990, they bought a house where they could live, rehearse, and screen-print their own T-shirts. Singer Wayne Coyne designed the four examples shown.

From the collection of Geoff Peveto

FLAMING LIPS
EYES

The Flaming Lips live up to the name of their early-years compilation, *Finally the Punk Rockers Are Taking Acid 1983–88.*

From the collection of Geoff Peveto

FLAMING LIPS
THE F.A.G.S.

"Give Yourself Some Head": a public service announcement from the FlAminGlipsS.

FLAMING LIPS
OKLAHOMA CITY

An eye-popping tribute to the band's hometown.

4. Beyond 2000

THE WHITE STRIPES
NOBODY KNOWS HOW TO TALK TO CHILDREN

From the collection of Ben Blackwell

"We didn't have enough spare cash in the first tours outside Detroit to print up real shirts. So we went to a dry goods store and bought softball team blank shirts—white with red sleeves, some with black sleeves. I taught myself to silk screen and borrowed some ink and did the shirts on my kitchen table. The backs said, 'Nobody knows how to talk to children,' which was/is the White Stripes' motto. It would be written in Latin on a scroll if we ever had a flag! Three colors, of course, red peppermints (the band's mascot), and black writing for the motto on the back. They were five bucks originally, as I remember. I think we sold the first one in Milwaukee. But I didn't make that many of them, maybe thirty."

—Jack White, The White Stripes

BONNIE "PRINCE" BILLY

Design by Marc Swanson.

SLEATER-KINNEY

Design by Marc Swanson.

THE DIRTBOMBS
PRAY FOR PILLS

"While driving through the Bowery
in 2002, the Dirtbombs came across a building repeatedly graffitied with the phrase 'Pray for Pills.' Agreeing with that sentiment, we called ahead to our Australian merch gurus (Love Police) and told them to design a T-shirt for our upcoming tour. Our only input was that it had to say 'Pray for Pills' on it. The actual pills in the corners and Thelonious Monk picture were just added brilliance. That same tour we recorded a live-to-acetate song at Corduroy Studios called 'Pray for Pills.' The phrase has quickly evolved from cryptic graffiti to band mantra."

—Ben Blackwell, The Dirtbombs

HOLLY GOLIGHTLY
SHARPY

Holly Golightly
Ko & The Knockouts
Original Criminals

"Basically, not being career-minded or very well organized, we forgot to order merch before a U.S. tour with Ko and the Knockouts and so [we] had to stop at a Wal-Mart to buy white T-shirts and marker pens. We drew them ourselves in the van on the way around on the tour, so every one is different and special to each city. The more we sold, the more we had to draw—it ate the miles up!" —Holly Golightly

From the collection of Dorien Garry

SILVER JEWS
PEACE

After releasing acclaimed albums for more than a decade, Silver Jews undertook their first-ever tour in spring 2006. This shirt comes from that tour.

From the collection of Courtney Shanks

MF DOOM
MASK

The MF stands for Metal Face and represents the metal mask MF DOOM is never seen without. Jeff Jank designed this shirt.

From the collection of Sean Nagin

ERASE ERRATA

T-shirt design by Jonathan Runcio.

From the collection of Courtney Shanks

EARLY MAN
HORSE

This fuzzy-skulled horse shirt was designed in 2006 by Wowch.

This is a beautiful use of the classic white-ink-on-black-shirt look. T-shirt design by Jake Manny.

GANG GANG DANCE

"This one was made using rubber stamps that friend/artist Oliver Payne made when he was doing a piece of animation for his contribution to the Gang Gang Dance DVD. I made a stencil with the letters G A N G and then just stamped up the negative space of the stencil with the 'dance' stamp. When we toured Australia, we hadn't made a screen for this one yet, so I would just sit in the hotel rooms and physically stamp them up by hand."

—Brian DeGraw, Gang Gang Dance

design made before our U.K. tour. It is the
simplest one, but the one I am most happy with so far.
The fist with the carrot is the logo for Food Not Bombs,
which has a sentimental connection to me from living in D.C.
in the early '90s. I was around a lot of grassroots, nonprofit
punk organizations/bands/crusty punks, etc., so it's always
nice nowadays when someone comments on it and
recognizes the logo. To me that means that they
have some sort of history of similar involvement."

—Brian DeGraw, Gang Gang Dance

215

BLACK DICE/BLOOD ON THE WALL

BLACK AND BLOOD

"This was a tour T-shirt we made for our very first tour. Black Dice had a hellish two-day tour—yes, two

days—that stretched all the way to Boston, then across the U.S.A. to North Hampton, and then back to New York. So we had to have merch to sell or we would starve and run out of gas. We made about forty of these

bad boys, and a lot of people wish we made more. A pot leaf says it all without saying too much."
—Brad Shanks, Black Dice/Blood on the Wall

From the collection of Courtney Shanks

BLOOD ON THE WALL
BOTW CREST

"I came up with the crest working behind a cash register. I doodled a lot. Some people say it is a lot like

the classic hardcore 'x' symbol, but I wanted it to look like a shield."

—Brad Shanks, Blood on the Wall

From the collection of Courtney Shanks

BLOOD ON THE WALL
HANDS

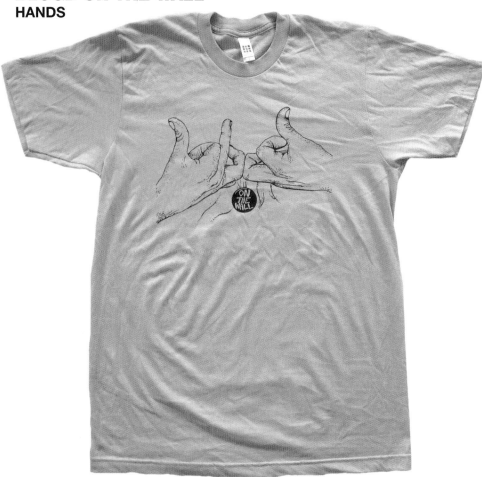

"This was designed by myself and our good friend J Penry. J Penry is my favorite artist in NYC, and he has helped us with flyers for years. We also used to slam dance a lot at shows. We were talking about what to do with the next BOTW T-shirt, and we thought it would be cool to have life-size hands spelling out 'blood.' I just hope a certain gang has a sense of humor about it and do not severely injure our fans, but I guess if they have to they can give out a light beat-down here and there. Maybe break their glasses and steal their iPod."

—Brad Shanks, Black Dice/Blood on the Wall

221

BLACK DICE
DOTS

This shirt is a still image from a band-created animation for a live show in 2002.

WOLF EYES
CLASSIC SNARL

223

This shirt, the Classic Snarl, has been sold on Wolf Eyes tours since 2000. It was designed by founding member Nathan Young.

YEAH YEAH YEAHS
MAPS

Featuring the lyrics to their love song "Maps," this shirt is from a 2006 U.S. tour. It was designed by Christian Joy, who is also responsible for singer Karen O's stage clothes.

225

Acknowledgments

Thanks to our friends, our family, and everybody
who contributed to the book.

Thanks to Jeff Sheinkopf for his obsessive attention to detail,
Ben Blackwell for his winning personality and conversational skills,
and Kelly Gibney for her big mouth.

Special thanks to
Michael Nagin, Jane Archer, Tricia Boczkowski,
Terra Chalberg, and Patrick Price.

INDEX OF FEATURED ARTISTS

HENRY OLIVER played in the band Die! Die! Die! and designed their album covers and T-shirts.

AMBER EASBY has worked for bands such as the White Stripes and the Raconteurs as their merchandiser.